Let's Talk about Money Before You Tie the Knot

Let's Talk about Money Before You Tie the Knot

A Guide to Premarital Financial Counseling

JAMES H. WILSON

RESOURCE *Publications* · Eugene, Oregon

LET'S TALK ABOUT MONEY BEFORE YOU TIE THE KNOT
A Guide to Premarital Financial Counseling

ISBN 13: 978-1-55635-611-7

Manufactured in the U.S.A.
"Scripture quotations taken from the New American Standard Bible®
Copyright © 1960, 1962, 1963, 1968, 1971, 1972, 1973, 1975, 1977, 1995
by The Lockman Foundation. Used by permission." (www.Lockman.org)

*This book is dedicated
to my wife of fifty years, Mary.
She has been a helpmate
whose price is far above rubies.*

Contents

Preface

THIS MANUAL has been written to assist you as a couple preparing for marriage in the vital discussion of the financial issues that may cause difficulties later in your relationship. In studies of failed marriages, one issue emerges as a powerful causative agent: disagreements over finances.

In addition, we have touched on some issues that currently may be lacking in your life as a young married couple. This includes a number of life situations, such as the addition of children to the family. Too often financial provisions are considered after the fact rather than before, thus causing couples to miss out on what Einstein called the most powerful force in the universe: compound interest.

This workbook should become a valuable part of your permanent financial records with the goal of reviewing it every two or three years and updating it as your goals and objectives are modified. Such a review also helps you measure your progress. I caution you not to be discouraged by setbacks. Implementing and sustaining sound financial policies in the home requires commitment and practice. You can overcome failure by trying and trying again. In the words of Winston Churchill, "Never give up! Never give up! Never give up!" Keep trying to succeed with your financial planning. The rewards will be a more peaceful marriage and a better quality of life.

wife hath made herself ready.
8 And to her was granted that she
should be arrayed in fine linen,
clean and white: for the fine linen
is the righteousness of saints.

Acknowledgments

FOR SEVERAL years I have been praying for an opportunity to use my years of experience and training in the service of the church. Due to a client's marriage, I was presented with the opportunity to observe premarital counseling from the perspective of a financial planner. I was surprised to find out that little or nothing has been done in this area. Therefore, the idea for this book was born.

Many people served as encouragers in this project. The Reverend Dave McAuley first looked at the project and thought it had merit and offered several suggestions for improvement. The Reverend Larry Ball looked at the project and encouraged me to keep on with the effort and supplied the genesis for the title. Dr. Richard Ray also reviewed the manuscript and offered helpful suggestions.

I am also grateful to several pastors, the Reverend Tom Osterhaus, the Reverend David Wilson, and the Reverend Wade Coleman for actually field testing the project and also to the Reverend Bill Leuzinger for using the manual in counseling.

To Dr. Kenn Gangel and Dr. Mark Herring who went above and beyond "looking it over," I give my grateful appreciation.

For her patience in producing the many versions, I thank Jeanette Smith, and for help in selecting the graphics, my thanks go to Ann Chesser.

Finally, I must recognize the huge contribution of Gene Wigginton for his counsel, encouragement, and a listening ear.

James H. Wilson

Some Preliminaries

Personal financial planning and premarital financial counseling are kissing cousins. If you are contemplating marriage, whether for the first time, or following death or divorce, this small book will be a valuable resource, opening up discussions regarding individual attitudes and backgrounds about finances while informing readers of some basic and important principles.

Why Premarital Financial Counseling?

Money is the source of disagreement and dissolution of marriage as much as 56 percent of the time. Much potential family discord can be avoided through premarital financial planning, as certain issues are raised and attitudes explored regarding the use of financial resources. The Bible mentions stewardship and money more frequently than any other single topic. Let's explore some basic scriptural foundations for handling money.

The five Scripture verses listed below serve to highlight the importance of personal financial planning. These verses go to the heart of man, which the Bible describes as basically sinful (Jer 17:9). This sinful heart, unless changed by a new relationship with God through Jesus Christ's shed blood, offers a worst-case scenario for settling money matter discord in marriage. Even among Christians financial management is a difficult task. The following verses were selected to deal with our baser instincts and to remind us that we have a higher calling to work out our differences.

The first verse we want to look at is from Genesis. It is often described as the Cultural Mandate, for in it, God commanded man to have dominion over the earth. But with this command came great responsibility:

> And God blessed them; and God said to them, "Be fruitful and multiply, and fill the earth, and subdue it; and rule over the fish of the sea and over the birds of the sky, and over every living thing that moves on the earth" (Gen 1:28).

The Lord gave the parents of the human race the mandate to rule, but Eve decided to disobey God by believing her own and her husband Adam's perceptions. Thus, man fell and sin entered the world in all its manifest forms. The verse below from 1 John emphasizes more than sexual connotations. For example, the lust of the flesh is interpreted by many commentators to mean a lust for comfort and luxury, while the lust of the eyes has to do with a covetous attitude. The "boastful pride of life" is equated with raw, unhealthy ambition. If these factors motivate our lives, then we will be failures in the matter of stewardship:

> For all that is in the world, the lust of the flesh and the lust of the eyes and the boastful pride of life, is not from the Father, but is from the world" (1 John 2:16).

In 1 Timothy, the Apostle Paul gives us helpful guidelines about attitudes towards money. Notice that the love of money is the root of all kinds of evil—not just money itself, which is essentially neutral. Again, as with most of our lives, attitude is the important element. Please remember—money is only a medium of exchange—and nothing more!

> And if we have food and covering with these we shall be content. But those who want to get rich fall into temptation and a snare and many foolish and harmful desires which plunge men into ruin and destruction. For the love of money is a root of all sorts of evil, and some by longing for it have wandered away from the faith, and pierced themselves with many a pang (1 Tim 6: 8–10).

The responsibility to provide for our own families should motivate us to pursue good financial planning, hence good stewardship. The following verse illustrates that point:

> But if anyone does not provide for his own, and especially for those of his household, he has denied the faith, and is worse than an unbeliever (I Tim 5:8).

If we look around it is easy to find people who are worse off financially than we are. The Bible clearly teaches God's people that they are obligated to help the poor. In the Old Testament the Israelites were instructed to leave rows of grain unpicked and leave grain on the sides for people to glean. Paul re-emphasizes that we need to share from our bounty with those less fortunate:

> Now this I say, he who sows sparingly shall also reap sparingly; and he who sows bountifully shall also reap bountifully. Let each one do just as he has purposed in his heart; not grudgingly or under compulsion (2 Cor 9:6–7).

The five verses listed above can be condensed as follows:

- Put God first
- Take care of your family
- Provide for your older years by saving now
- Adopt a healthy attitude about material possessions
- Develop a generous spirit

These five points will go a long way in establishing the direction and soundness of your financial planning.

The third reason for premarital financial counseling is to discover differences now so they can be addressed before your vows are said. Through such open discussion, you as a couple may grow deeper together in understanding financial values, plans, and priorities. Possibly you may decide that because of wide differences in attitudes toward money, spending habits, and other factors, the union may not be right for you. If so, it may be a short-term tragedy but one that will actually result in long-term benefits for both of you.

What is Premarital Financial Counseling?

Premarital financial counseling attempts to discover individual attitudes and thoughts about material possessions. Through this process we will seek to explore family financial backgrounds and the attitudes that parents and grandparents had regarding their financial resources.

Finally, through counseling, we hope to offer solutions, not just raise problems and/or issues. Solutions will be discussed in response to significant questions, such as the following:

- What is debt reduction?
- How much should we spend for a house?
- What kind of insurance do we need?
- What are some key financial aspects of having children?
- When and how should we begin preparing for retirement?
- How do we plan to pay for children's college in the future?

How Do We Go About Premarital Financial Counseling?

Counselors need good materials in the form of questionnaires, financial statements, and discussion questions. It is also helpful to have explanatory text to give reasons why certain measures are recommended or included for discussion.

Premarital financial counseling involves discussions with a knowledgeable counselor. This may be a pastor or layman who has been assigned the role by the minister performing the wedding ceremony. It should be noted that counseling should be done well in advance of your wedding. A wise attorney I have worked with in the past has suggested, particularly in the case of developing premarital agreements[1] for second marriages, that all financial counseling be done *before* the wedding date is set. This is extremely wise advice and should be heeded, particularly by those of you who are contemplating marriage.

Finally, premarital financial counseling involves discussions between both of you. A frank and open exchange of opinions and ideas is essential. This is the keystone to a successful archway which will, from a financial standpoint, hold up the building of your marriage.

---

1. See Appendix 1 for a broader discussion of premarital agreements.

The remainder of this book will be divided into three sections—the Past, the Present, and the Future. The past shapes our attitudes for the present. The present sets forth the predicate for the future. The future expresses our hopes, dreams, goals, and objectives. It is my hope that this will be a helpful guide and a thought-provoking exercise, especially as we keep in mind the spiritual dimension. Marriage was instituted by God, as revealed in the book of Genesis, and should be entered into with much prayer, thought and planning:

> And the Lord God fashioned into a woman the rib which He had taken from the man, and brought her to the man. And the man said, "This is now bone of my bones, and flesh of my flesh: She shall be called Woman. Because she was taken out of Man." For this cause a man shall leave his father and his mother, and shall cleave to his wife; and they shall become one flesh (Gen 2:22–24).

Let's do what is required to follow the biblical principle of achieving oneness—for our purposes, in the area of managing wealth according to God's design.

2

The Past

REVISITING OUR past can be a healthy, productive exercise. Let me caution you at this point to avoid dwelling on failures or successes but instead to merely review the past with the idea of learning from both positive and negative experiences in order to make your marriage more successful.

Several questions regarding the past emerge which you and your fiancée should do your best to answer. The first has to do with your childhood, including such things as your parents, their education, their work, your family lifestyle, religious beliefs, and even such things as the frequency of family vacations. These will be viewed from the financial impact viewpoint since each item involves not only relationship issues but also effects on the family budget.

For example, if one of you had parents who were well-educated and employed in financially-rewarding occupations, while the other came from a more humble background, this should be a point of discussion because your view of finances may be shaped greatly by your childhood experience.

Many times it is extremely difficult for the children of well-to-do families to adapt to the more humble beginnings that most young married people face. Your expectations of where you are going to live, what kind of cars you will drive, or what clothes you can afford cannot be shaped by the past but must be formed by the present. This saw cuts both ways. Those individuals from humble beginnings often have a difficult time adjusting to new-found financial well-being. It also can result in pent-up spending sprees which are a cause for family discord.

The second question relates to the subject of previous marriages. From a financial standpoint, if you or your partner bring into a new marriage financial responsibilities from a former alliance, that should be looked at and discussed with a realistic view of what the impact will be upon your current financial situation. Responsibilities for alimony and child support put a strain on a future relationship, not only financially, but also psychologically, as your new spouse may resent the diversion of resources to another family. These are matters that should be discussed openly and freely and looked at realistically in light of your current financial situation.

The question of bankruptcy arises because it is becoming more and more prevalent in our society, even among Christians. If one of you has declared bankruptcy, this is a red flag to be examined carefully. It is important to consider all the circumstances involved with bankruptcy and to determine why it was necessary. From a Christian viewpoint, bankruptcy should be considered as a court of last resort. Even if this measure is taken to relieve pressures, the debts forgiven in the process should not be ignored by the bankrupt Christian. Every effort should be made to repay those obligations, even though the individual has been legally absolved of responsibility. Bankruptcy is really a form of stealing if the debt is never repaid. Anyone entering into bankruptcy has a moral obligation to repay his or her debts, even if not legally required to do so.

While the question of pre-existing health problems is sensitive and should be approached with consideration, it nevertheless is an important factor in the marriage and has financial ramifications. The possibility of inheriting genes that produced those health problems should be looked at. Since the marriage contract is for better or worse, and in sickness and in health, potential problems related to health should be viewed realistically in light of the financial impact they will have upon your prospective union. This is not cause for calling off the wedding, but it can be a signal for you as a couple to make advance preparations with guidance from health care professionals to mitigate problems.

Work experience is important in everyone's life. If one of you has contributed toward your own support for a long period of time while the other has been given material benefits without working for them, these differences should be discussed in light of the future financial relationship between the two of you. Former experiences regarding the value of work can be instrumental in shaping our future view of work and work ethic. My wife and I have three children, and each of them began working in the teen years at jobs such as clerking in department stores, waiting tables, being a bag boy at the supermarket, etc. All of these experiences were valuable in helping them develop a good work ethic. While work experience is certainly beneficial, other factors shape our attitudes toward the value and use of money. Therefore, additional mentoring is necessary.

The use of credit cards affords one of the great social and financial challenges of the day. Credit cards should be used only as a convenience—not as a means of financing purchases. If you can't pay off your credit card at the end of the month, don't use it. Buying on credit can be addictive. I have counseled with several people who used credit cards to ease their purchase of items which they really could not afford, resulting in serious marital problems. As a couple preparing for marriage, you should make full disclosure to each other as to your use of credit and credit cards.

If you have attended college, the two of you should discuss how your schooling was financed, particularly if you borrowed under a student loan program. Many times people graduate from college owing thousands of dollars in educational loans. These can sometimes equal the value of a mortgage on a house. Investigate opportunities to consolidate school loans and lessen the financial drain upon family resources. In any event, full disclosure should be made regarding debt of this nature.

Using a checking account or debit card can be a valuable tool for financial education. I think it is a good idea for young people to have checking accounts at an early age. Make sure before you get married that each of you knows how to use a checking account and how to balance and reconcile the account at the end of every month. It is also important for you to agree as to who will be responsible for paying the monthly bills. The decision shouldn't be based on gender, but rather on whom you both recognize as the best equipped to faithfully perform this duty.

Finally, what is your experience in budgeting? People often react strongly when the word *budget* is mentioned, even to the point of going ballistic, as I have observed during certain counseling sessions.

While there are many different ways to establish a family budget, the important thing is to do something. The best way to determine this is to have a frank assessment of each party's past financial history, including experience with budgeting. In the next section, the Present, you will find suggestions to help you devise an effective budget.

Questions for Discussion

1. What are the greatest financial differences in each partner's past?

    _____

    _____

2. How do you see both differences and similarities from your past affecting how you approach financial matters in your marriage?

    _____

    _____

3. If one or both of you have been previously married, have you settled the potential problems resulting in any carryovers from those former unions?

    _____

    _____

4. As to health problems, are you ready to say and mean "in sickness and in health"?

    _____

    _____

5. Will the presence of formal education (or a lack thereof) create difficulties for you in the future?

    _____

    _____

6. If you are bringing a large debt load into the marriage, have you developed a plan to deal with it?

    _____

    _____

7. Describe your childhood. Include such things as parents' education, work, family lifestyle, religious beliefs, vacations, etc.

8. Have you ever declared bankruptcy? If so, what restitution have you made or are you making?

9. Describe work experiences you've had.

10. Have you had credit cards? If yes, list them and explain your views regarding how they should be used. *Have you followed in practice what you have described?*

11. If you attended college, how was your schooling paid for?

12. Have you had a checking account?

13. Have you been accustomed to budgeting your expenses?

14. What kind of house(s) did you live in?

    _____

    _____

15. What kind of cars did your parents drive? How long did they keep them?

    _____

    _____

3

The Present

DURING OUR last session we explored the past, trying to zero in on those items in your financial history that would affect the present and the future. In this section we will look at your current financial situation.

We have provided worksheets in appendix 1 giving you space to list your assets and liabilities (what you own and what you owe), and an opportunity to prepare a budget for your household-to-be.

First, let's address the list of assets and liabilities. Assets refer to anything you own, whether tangible items such as cars and furniture, or intangible, such as stocks, mortgages, copyrights, or patents. These items should be listed not at cost but at their fair market value. Does this mean you must go out and get appraisals? No, just give it your best shot as far as your understanding of current value is concerned. On the liability side take stock of items such as credit card debt, real estate mortgages, and school loans. You can list these on the form provided and then subtract the amount of liabilities from the total amount of assets to see if there is any net worth.

It is possible for a young couple recently graduated from college to have a negative net worth because of school loans and other debt. If this is the case, then you should consider these as prime targets to take aim at as soon as possible. However, if you very low interest rates on the school loans, you may want to take advantage of that feature. While it is good to be debt-free, you don't want to be in a position of sacrificing the present for the future. By this I mean that it is entirely possible to keep debt in proper prospective and at the same time have money to live on and not to be scrimping and saving beyond what is reasonable. There is a fine balance, and with good financial counseling, you should be able to attain it.

This can best be illustrated by a story about a client of mine who was adamantly opposed to debt. He was so opposed that he deprived his family of certain basic living standards. For example, the kitchen floor was rotting away and the appliances were in a sad state of disrepair. But he was making double and triple principal payments on the house mortgage. After we engaged in some heart-to-heart consultations, he realized he was being over-zealous in his approach to debt management and was persuaded to reduce his mortgage payments so there was cash flow available to renovate the kitchen.

Preparing the Budget

Perhaps you are asking, "What exactly is a household budget and how do we go about preparing one?" Let's start off by saying that *budget* is not a dirty word. (See the glossary for the definition of this term.) Done properly and kept in proper perspective, a budget can be a life-saving financial plan for you. The forms provided in this book will lead you through the development of such a plan. Keep in mind that a budget is not written in stone. It is a malleable document that should change over time as you get a better handle on your expenses. A sample budget has been provided to give you an idea of how a couple with a certain amount of income will budget that income in proper amounts. (Note sample budget included in appendix 1.)

For the purpose of our budget projections, let us consider a hypothetical couple who has purchased a condo, having been given the down payment by their parents. They have a mortgage of $50,000 for thirty years and hope to start a family after three years of marriage with the wife working part-time from the home. They also have a car loan that will be paid off in three years. They intend for the budget surpluses from the first three years to be saved as a rainy day fund to be applied toward the time when they eventually have one income.

I would like to emphasize a couple of items here. First, in preparing a workable budget, we must keep in mind the timing of the income. Let's assume that the couple is paid on a bi-weekly basis (every two weeks). Second, we should consider that a recently-married couple may be renting rather than purchasing a house or condo. But in either event, purchase or rent, the total cost of housing should not exceed thirty percent of their net take-home pay. Remember, that is the upper limit. Make every attempt to keep it under thirty percent. More will be said about this when we get to question seven of this section dealing with budgeting housing expenses.

The item entitled "Asset Replacement" under "Somewhat Discretionary Expenses" is intended to enable you to prepare financially for the unexpected. In a perfect world, you would be able to put these discretionary funds into a savings account or money market fund and use them for unexpected emergency expenditures such a car repair or replacement of appliances. In our hypothetical budget the couple has a balance of $400 plus per month which should be left over after budgeting for expenses. However, usually these hypothetical surpluses do not exist, at least not in the amount shown on paper. A computer program such as Quicken can help you keep track of your monthly expenditures.

I encourage you to attack these two exercises as the first step in dealing with your present financial status. List your assets and liabilities, and then prepare a budget.

School Loans

If you have debt from attending college or post graduate education, you would do well to explore the possibility of consolidating the loans and selecting an appropriate time period to amortize the debt. Again, I caution you not to sacrifice present-day living with an obsession of getting out of debt.

The Cost of the Wedding

I have seen many couples spend a small fortune—either theirs or their parents' on the wedding. How much to spend on this momentous event is a question of values shared by you and your spouse-to-be which should be discussed openly with both sets of parents. Each of you should be prepared with a projection of wedding costs and method of payment. If you have wealthy parents who can afford to pay for an expensive wedding, you may want to discuss reducing the cost and using some of that money as a down payment on a house, for deposit into a savings account, or for reduction of school loans.

As part of your preparation for wedding expenses, you should have a budget outlining the major expenditures. As you prepare this budget, be sure you do not omit gratuities, especially the one for the minister. I have talked to several pastors one who told me they were either given no honorarium or a ridiculously small one. If you consider that the minister has spent five or six hours in premarital counseling and then gives the better part of two days at the wedding rehearsal dinner and the wedding itself and, of course, if it is out of town that adds even more time—and then to be given short shrift violates the principle that the laborer is worthy of his hire.

At the date of this writing, I suggest a minimum honorarium of $200 for the biblical performance of the ceremony plus expenses the minister may incur. If you consider the equivalent time spent (including the counseling time) at the professional rates a lawyer or accountant would charge, the "fee" would be well in excess of $1,000. So let me repeat, please consider the minister as you set your budget.

The honeymoon can also be an occasion for excessive spending, and while the memories may be lasting, the question must be asked, is it worth it to have lasting debt? This entire section is a plea for moderation. It will serve you well in the future if you plan your wedding and honeymoon sensibly. Make pleasant memories, but keep the finances in mind so you avoid a debtor's regret.

Whose Career Will You Follow?

Assuming there are no children involved, you each will probably be working. You should sit down and discuss whose career will be primary. In most instances it will be the male's. Set up your budget so you can live on one income and save as much as possible from the second income for the day when children arrive or for some other major event you have planned for.

Insurance

Usually young couples have not considered the need for insurance. At marriage all of this changes and you have to start thinking of each other in the event of your disability or death. Let's discuss the types of insurance one by one.

Life Insurance

At the beginning of a marriage, life insurance is not usually a large problem, although you must be sure to have a reserve of funds for burial in the event of death. Because life insurance is so inexpensive at early ages, it might be well to get a certain base amount that will carry you through the event of having children and benefits to carry the children through college. I normally recommend to clients that they consider level premium term insurance.

Essentially there are only two types of life insurance: *permanent insurance* wherein you give the insurance company not only the mortality and administrative costs, but also additional money that the insurance company invests for you. This is usually not the best type of insurance to carry.

The other type is *term insurance*, and the premium essentially covers the insurance company's costs of mortality and administration. Term insurance is the least expensive and when taken out at an early age gives you the most value. Please note that it is not only the husband but the wife as well who needs insurance. By going on the Internet you can research the costs of level premium term insurance. You should be able to find a local agent who can come close to matching the quotes you get online. I usually advise that you have a local agent because of the helpful advice and service you can obtain from him or her.

Initially you may want to think in terms of a twenty-year or twenty-five year level premium term policy for the husband in the amount of $250,000 and another term policy of $250,000 on the wife. One rule of thumb to determine how much life insurance you need is five to ten times earnings, depending upon age and family circumstances.

However, you should actually fill out an insurance needs analysis. This can be done with the help of a good financial counselor.

Health Insurance

Usually health insurance is provided by employers but because of its expense, they are finding it more difficult to supply. I advise you to look into health savings accounts now being marketed. Once again, you should engage an accountant, CPA or good financial advisor to discuss this with you.

Disability Income Insurance

This coverage is often overlooked. Most folks can afford to die and they can afford to live, but they cannot afford to become disabled. Many times disability insurance is provided through your employer, but often it is not. If not, you should investigate private disability insurance and buy as much as you can afford. Normally you can cover about sixty percent of your income through disability insurance.

Auto, Property, and Casualty Insurance

If you own automobiles and a house, you will want to have the proper amount of liability coverage, including an "umbrella policy." An umbrella policy is an excess liability policy sold in increments of $1,000,000 coverage. Unless you have children who are drivers, the cost of this umbrella policy is usually modest. Also, you should look at the deductibles for your property, homeowner's, and auto insurance, and take the largest deductible you feel you can afford. This will have a salutary effect on the premium charged. The larger the deductible, the less the premium.

Homeowner or Renter Insurance

If you are renting your home, you need renter's insurance to cover liability and theft. This type insurance is often overlooked, particularly by young couples, but it is extremely important to acquire as protection from losses due to damage and theft.

Budgeting for Housing Expenses

Housing expenses include the rent or mortgage payment, utilities, property taxes, and insurance and condo fees. The total of these expenses should not exceed thirty percent of your net income. Again, I say that this should be the upside amount; the lower, the better with respect to housing costs.

When you start out, the decision of whether to rent to buy is often dictated by whether you have money for the down payment. But beyond that, other considerations should be taken into account. For example, if you know you will be in a community for only a brief period of time—one to three years—it is not wise to buy a house.

A house is considered to be an illiquid (not easily converted to cash) asset, and depending upon the real estate market, may or may not sell promptly. Moreover, when you sell a house, you usually go through a realtor, adding a six percent selling cost to the disposal of the property. I have counseled with many couples regarding this item, and they usually come back and thank me for suggesting that they rent. After experiencing a sudden need to move, they welcomed the freedom of not having to worry about selling a house.

Young couples often struggle over how much to invest in a residence. I have several rules of thumb which depend upon finances at the time of the investment. The first rule is that you should restrict the purchase price of the house to no more than two times your annual earnings. So if you earn $60,000 per year, your housing cost should not exceed $120,000. Remember, these are the *upper* limits for determining how much to spend.

In another situation you may have substantial net worth and be able to afford much more than two times your annual earnings. In this instance I would recommend that you limit your investment in a residence to no more than twenty-five percent of your available net worth.

As a final guideline, I would say that your monthly housing costs should not exceed thirty percent of your net take-home pay. You can use one or more of these rules to determine how much to spend on a house. The main idea is not to become a slave to brick and mortar.

A final thought about entering the house market is the suggestion that you look into condos as opposed to free-standing family residences. Young couples often find it much easier to get into the condo market because they are less expensive than houses. Once again, remember that the *primary rule in real estate is location, location, location.* So even when buying a condo, choose an area that has promise for future appreciation.

Your View of Debt

I encourage each of you to discuss and describe your view of debt. Debt can be a terrible taskmaster, but if controlled it can also work to your benefit enabling you to acquire assets which will enhance your quality of life. Therefore, you should go into the marriage having a healthy attitude about debt and understanding that you must control it, because once it gets out of the bottle, the genie can be extremely harsh. Master the concept of deferred gratification. You don't always need a brand new car right now. You don't need the most expensive furniture. You don't need the highest lifestyle. In fact, I recommend that many of you, particularly professionals, always live two years behind your income. In other words don't anticipate income or even try to live up to the income that you presently have. Take time to get settled, grounded, and comfortable with your family budget.

Contributions to the Work of God

It has often been said that you should pay God first and yourself second. I would concur with that based on the teaching of Scripture.

> "Bring the whole tithe into the storehouse, so that there may be food in My house, and test Me now in this," says the Lord of hosts, "if I will not open for you the windows of heaven, and pour out for you a blessing until it overflows" (Mal 3:10).

Discuss together what percentage of income you plan to give to the Lord's work, and settle the matter before you marry. Early in my professional life I advised a Christian client in matters concerning his estate and noticed he had a separate bank account for his charitable contributions. This is not only an excellent vehicle for segregating your tithes and offerings, but it also has a psychological effect of freeing you from ownership of those funds.

Questions about the Present

1. On the worksheets provided (see appendix 1):

    a. List your assets and liabilities

    _____

    _____

    b. Prepare a budget for your household

2. If you have school loans, have you explored the possibility of consolidating the loans?

    _____

    _____

3. Do you have a budget for the cost of the wedding? Who is paying these costs?

    _____

    _____

4. Have you considered the cost of the honeymoon and how you will pay for it?

    _____

    _____

5. Will you each be working? Describe your jobs and estimated income.

    _____

    _____

6. Have you considered the need for insurance?

   a. Life

   b. Health

   c. Disability

   d. Auto, property and casualty

   e. Homeowner's or renter's

7. Do you know how much of your budget you should allocate to housing expenses? Housing expenses include:

   a. Rent or mortgage payment

   b. Utilities

   c. Property taxes

   d. Insurance

   e. Property owner's association fees

8. Describe your view of debt. Include thoughts about how debt should be used, to what extent it should be included in your budget, the concept of deferred gratification, etc.

   _____

   _____

9. Do you believe in and practice tithing?

   _____

   _____

10. What is your attitude about automobiles? List the details of automobiles currently owned.

    _____

    _____

4

The Future

Goals and Objectives

Now that we have looked at the past and present, it is time to look to the future. You will find an appendix sheet to help you with setting goals and objectives for at least the next five years. This worksheet is intended to be a primer to prod your thinking in terms of planning for the future. It is not an end in itself.

People who are goal-oriented accomplish more and do it in a more orderly fashion than those who do not engage in planning. While it takes time to develop a good plan, the overall time to achieve a goal is cut a lot shorter by such projections.

Where to Live and Work

After you have finished setting goals and objectives, you should include where you want to live and work, at least for the foreseeable future. In some instances this is already decided for you—say, if you are going on for graduate study or if there is a work-required relocation. Absent those restrictions, research areas of the country where you will want to live and work. Ample studies are available regarding all facets of various geographical locations, everything from crime to medical care. Some of you may be oriented toward urban living while others prefer rural or suburban living. It becomes an individual choice, assuming there is work available in each location. One last point—don't forget your extended family. Some people consider it essential to be close to family while others wish to be as far away as possible. This is something that should be factored into your decision and determined long before the wedding day.

Having Children

If you and your spouse-to-be-are of child-bearing age, you have to answer the question of children. What are your feelings about having children? What is your philosophy regarding one parent staying at home to care for the children after they are born versus the use of daycare centers? You should keep in mind that daycare costs can financially negate the benefits of working. The relationship with the child can also be disrupted. Before you have children, the area of care should be explored and a decision reached. The cost of raising one child including the cost of college education can reach into the tens if not hundreds of thousands of dollars. Offsetting this is the biblical admonition that children are a blessing of the Lord and make a couple, a family (Psalm 127). Both of you should be of one mind when it comes to this matter. How many children you plan to have should be discussed thoroughly before you marry.

Children's Education

If you decide that children are in your future, you must consider early on, the expense of a college education if indeed this is a path you wish for your child to follow. If so, you need to ask, how will his or her education be financed? Half facetiously and half seriously I have always said the best way to finance a child's college education is to have wealthy grandparents. Frequently grandparents do wish to help, and the easiest thing to do in this regard is to use one of the tax provisions that have been provided for saving for higher education. Grandparents can pay tuition directly to the school and not be exposed to gift tax or generation-skipping tax. Other options could include a Coverdell Educational Savings Account or a Section 529 Plan. A CPA or personal financial planner can fill you in on the details of these two plans, but they are very effective and can be used to great benefit if started at the birth of a child. See appendix 1 for a brief description of these plans.

Rainy Day Fund

Having a rainy day fund set aside for the inevitable contingencies and emergencies that arise in life is essential in your personal financial plan. I usually recommend that you have three to six months of normal living expenses set aside for such contingencies. Many times people do not have these funds readily available, but if you start saving from your income (make sure that this is your first priority) before investment and even before fully funding retirement plans, you should be able to build a reserve. For individuals with high incomes, a line of credit from your bank can replace the need for cash savings. This permits more cash to be available for debt reduction.

Retirement of Debt

As part of your future financial plan, you need a plan to retire debt. Many young people coming out of college have substantial school debt or credit card debt. There should be open discussion and mutual agreement as to how this debt is going to be handled in your marriage as we saw in the last section. See appendix 1 for an apt illustration.

Inheritances

Some people anticipate inheritance as an integral part of their own financial plan. This is not a good idea. If you happen to get an inheritance somewhere along the way in life, count it as an added blessing, but I would recommend planning based upon zero possibility of an inheritance. The other side of inheritance may be seen when grown children must provide assistance to elderly parents. If this is the case with you, be sure to discuss it with your intended spouse.

Retirement

Thinking about retirement is good up to a point. However, do not become so absorbed with future retirement that you sacrifice your present living standard. As with most things in life, there is a happy balance. The earlier you start saving for the ultimate goal of financial independence, the better. Included in appendix 1 is an illustration of how an early saver can accumulate much more income than one who starts later in life. This is a dramatic illustration of the power of compound interest.

As you can see, there are many things to think about regarding future planning before you wed. I recommend that you do a sufficient amount of planning, but not to the point that it becomes obsessive-compulsive behavior. Then quarterly, sit down as a couple and review your financial plan to ascertain the progress you have made thus far. If you have failed in certain areas, don't be discouraged. You can always start again. This is an instance where something is better than nothing. So with this encouragement, I wish you well as you embark on the sea of matrimony.

Wills, Powers of Attorney and Living Wills

Make an appointment with an attorney even before marriage to lay out the parameters of a will and durable powers of attorney for general business, as well as for health care and a living will.

A will not only directs the disposal of assets but also covers such things as guardianship for minor children, the possibility of setting up trusts, and the naming of those beneficiaries that are the objects of the testator's bounty. An instrument not quite so familiar is a durable power of attorney. This document enables one person to give legal authority to another to act on another's behalf. "Durable" means that the person so designated can act when the principal loses capacity.

A healthcare power of attorney is very similar to a durable power of attorney but directed exclusively at healthcare concerns.

A living will is written instruction that allows you to spell out your medical treatment wishes (usually about life support) if you become unable to speak for yourself.

These are important documents and should be considered as you enter into marriage.

Family Notebook

Several years ago I set up a three-ring notebook for my wife so she could know where our major assets were and what the major assets were in the event of my death or incapacity.

You may be interested in doing something similar for your spouse. Buy a regular three-ring notebook with dividers. In the front, create an index showing what contents are found under each divider. For example, the index would have a list of key papers and identify where they are located. Those items to be considered are as follows:

1. Life insurance policies and long-term health care insurance

2. Copies of wills, etc.

3. Any major contracts that are income producing

4. Pension papers

5. Property and casualty insurance

6. Safe deposit box location and contents

7. Copies of recent tax returns

In this notebook you could also put copies of broker statements and a narrative as to the value of your house and other real estate and maybe even instructions regarding professional advisors to contact in the event of death or incapacity of either spouse.

Please note: Keep the notebook under lock and key!

The family notebook will not only be helpful to your spouse but also to the advisors that must assist him or her. It takes very little time to set up such a file, yet it can save many hours should an emergency arise. This is a good process to go through regardless of age or marital status because it gives you a chance to review your important documents and get yourself organized. So don't wait. Start today!

Questions about the Future

1. Using the worksheet provided, list your goals and objectives for the next five years. (See appendix 1.)

2. Where do you plan to live and work?

   _____

   _____

3. Are you planning to have children?

   a. If yes, can you live on one income?

   b. If yes, is it your hope that they attend college?

   c. If yes, how will you pay for the costs of a college education?

4. Will you set aside systematic savings for a rainy day fund?

   _____

   _____

5. Have you contacted a lawyer to have wills, powers of attorney, and living wills prepared?

   _____

   _____

6. Will you set up family financial notebook?

   _____

   _____

Facilitators Guide

Overview of the Assignment

YOU ARE acting as a facilitator to an engaged couple in the review of financial matters pending their forthcoming marriage. Your primary role is to ensure that the manual is used properly and that the discussion stays on track so the financial matters will be properly addressed.

You are also responsible for remaining neutral so as to not impose your ideas on the couple. This means that you are to be a good listener—the interpreter of the material in the manual. Consider your role more in the nature of a coach. The succeeding pages will take each part of the manual and try to give you helpful hints as the facilitator regarding the conduct of the meetings and some key thoughts and high points to be emphasized in the material.

In the case of older couples who have been married before, the questions and approach can be modified accordingly, but essentially the same areas should be covered. In addition, you should call their attention to the section in appendix 1, "Pros and Cons of Premarital Agreements." This is extremely important for older people to address because there may be children on both sides who have to be considered.

The suggested time frame for meetings is listed below.

PROPOSED SCHEDULE

Meeting #1	30 minutes
Meeting #2	45 minutes
Meeting #3	45 minutes
Meeting #4	45 minutes

Ideally the meetings should be spaced one week apart.

First Meeting—30 minutes

During the first meeting you will ask the participants to peruse the manual, looking with broad strokes at everything from the preface to the preliminaries to the three main parts and the appendices.

It is incumbent upon you at this point to encourage candor and honesty as financial matters are laid on the table for discussion.

After reviewing the manual and its contents, begin the first chapter, "Some Preliminaries," and emphasize the following points:

1. The major reason for disagreement and dissolution of marriage is money-related at least fifty-six percent of the time.

2. Review the five scripture verses to see if you can ascertain if the candidates are in accord with a biblical approach.

3. Review the summary and key items.

4. Review the main points of premarital financial counseling as listed in the text.

5. Explain the process that will be followed during the counseling sessions.

   In preparation for the next meeting, ask the participants to read chapter 2. Go over the "Questions about the Past" and have each party answer these for the next meeting by writing them out as short answers.

The Past

Second Meeting—45 minutes

Go over the written answers to the questions assigned to the couple from the last meeting.

Key Points in "Questions about the Past":

- Question 8—You should ascertain if either party has ever been through bankruptcy or even contemplated bankruptcy.

- Question 10—has a big impact upon the financial well-being of a family. You should thoroughly explore how each party uses credit cards.

- Question 11—Determine if there is a school debt that could pose a problem financially for the couple.

- Questions 14 and 15 have to do with expectations for the future based upon the couple's past experience.

This section offers questions for discussion. These are very important and should not be sloughed off. Make sure each party contributes to the discussion, and satisfy yourself that they have resolved any differences that may arise.

Go over the worksheets for assets and liabilities, and budgeting.

Ask the couple to read the next section, "The Present," and answer the "Questions about the Present."

The Present

Third Meeting—45 minutes

Go over the written answers to questions assigned from the last session. Cover the sample budget to see how it stacks up against their proposed budget.

Key points in "Questions about the Past":

- Question 3 is very important for determining how the couple views material items. The cost of the wedding can tell you a great deal about their value system as far as money is concerned. Stress the need to have a decent honorarium for the minister performing the wedding. See the sample letter in appendix 2.

- Question 4 is related to question 3 as far as what it will tell you.

- With question 6 you can look through the text regarding insurance, and cover each item with the couple.

- The information for question 7 is found in the text, but you should have the couple consider how it compares to their own budget.

- Question 8 is very important in the sense that you can get insights into the couple's view of handling debt and whether or not special help is needed in that area.

- Question 9 has to do with their spiritual understanding of tithing.

- Question 10 will also give you a clue as to their view of material possessions.

Assign the next section, "The Future," and have the couple answer the questions.

The Future

Fourth Meeting—45 minutes

Again, the participants should have worked through the questions and worksheets prior to the meeting.

Key Points:

- Question 3 will determine if they can live on one income and reveal what their idea is about children and a stay-at-home spouse.

- Question 4 talks about systematic savings and again will give you an idea of their view of financial responsibility (refer to appendix 1 to show how savings works).

- In question 5 it should be stressed that the couple contact an attorney and have these documents prepared for execution after their marriage.

- Question 6 introduces the financial family notebook. Review the subject matter in the text so they understand how the notebook should be constructed.

Review the entire program and encourage questions regarding the material covered.

Appendix 1

Personal Profile

Statement of Net Worth

Details of Debt

Debt Management—Details of Debt

Budget Information

Budget Projections

Goals and Objectives

Time Value of Money

Premarital Agreements

College Savings Plans

Personal Profile

GENERAL INFORMATION   Date _____

Your Full Name _____

Your Place of Birth _____

Date of Birth _____

Citizenship _____

Present Address _____

_____

_____

Home Phone _____   E-Mail _____

Work Phone _____   E-Mail _____

Cell Phone _____

FAMILY INFORMATION:

    Father's Name _____

    Deceased?   Yes _____   No _____

    If deceased, date and cause of death _____

    Mother's Name _____

    Deceased?   Yes _____   No _____

    If deceased, date and cause of death

    Any familial health problems? _____

    _____

    _____

CURRENT EMPLOYMENT:

Company	Position	Year of Employment

Please give a brief description of education and work experience.

_____

_____

_____

_____

EXPECTED INHERITANCES

Source	Description	Estimated Value

Statement of Net Worth

<u>WHAT YOU OWN</u>   <u>AMOUNT TOTAL</u>

1. LIQUID ASSETS

Cash (Checking, Savings Accounts)   _____

Treasury Bills   _____

Savings Certificates   _____

Money Market Funds   _____

Cash Value of Life Insurance   _____

TOTAL LIQUID ASSETS   _____

2. INVESTMENT ASSETS

Marketable Securities: Stocks   _____

Marketable Securities: Bonds   _____

Real Estate (Investments)   _____

Retirement Funds   _____

TOTAL INVESTMENT ASSETS   _____

3. PERSONAL ASSETS

Residence   _____

Household Furnishings   _____

Art and Antiques   _____

Vehicles   _____

Boats   _____

Other Personal Assets   _____

TOTAL PERSONAL ASSETS   _____

TOTAL ASSETS   _____

TOTAL INVESTMENT ASSETS   _____

Statement of Net Worth

What You Owe	Amount	To Whom

4. SHORT-TERM OBLIGATIONS

Consumer Credit
Obligations   _____

Borrowings on Life
Insurance   _____

Installment Loans_____

Accrued Income Taxes_____

TOTAL Short-Term
Obligations   _____

5. LONG-TERM OBLIGATIONS

Loans: Investment
Assets   _____

Loans: Automobile_____

Loans: School   _____

Mortgage of Personal
Residence   _____

TOTAL Long-Term
Obligations   _____

TOTAL liabilities   _____

NET WORTH (Assets – Liabilities)   _____

DETAILS OF DEBT

Creditor	Date of Note	Original Amount	Current Balance	Monthly Payment	Interest Rate	Term of Loan

Debt Management

(An Example)

DETAILS OF DEBT

Creditor	Date of Note	Original Amount	Current Balance	Monthly Payment	Interest Rate	Term of Loan
Various credit cards			$20,000	$700	12.0%	33 mos.
School loans			$200,000	$1,000	3.88%	30 yrs.
Car loan			$20,000	$400	6.0%	60 mos.
Residence			$180,000	$1,326	6.25	30 yrs.

Dr. Smith and his wife, Sue, have been married for three years. They have one child and would like to have two more. Dr. Smith has been in practice for two years and earns $150,000 per year. Sue does not work. They have $25,000 in a savings account as a rainy day fund. The recommended strategy is as follows:

1. Get a line of credit from their bank to replace the $25,000 rainy day fund.

2. Use the $25,000 to pay off credit card debt.

3. Start making extra payments on their house mortgage and convert the payment from monthly to every two weeks (one-half of payment). This will reduce the life of the mortgage by six years, not counting the extra principal payments.

The general plan of attack is to pay off the highest interest debt first and then start reducing the house mortgage.

Budget Information

Item	Monthly Budget	Yearly Budget
1. EMPLOYMENT INCOME:		
Salary	_____	_____
TOTAL Employment Income	_____	_____
2. OTHER INCOME:		
Dividends and Interest	_____	_____
Other Income	_____	_____
TOTAL INCOME	_____	_____
3. INCOME TAXES:		
Income Taxes—Federal & State	_____	_____
Social Security	_____	_____
Other Deductions	_____	_____
TOTAL INCOME TAXES	_____	_____
4. COMMITTED EXPENDITURES:		
Housing (Mortgage/Rent)	_____	_____
Utilities and Telephone	_____	_____
Real Estate Taxes	_____	_____
Debt Repayment	_____	_____
Property and Liability Insurance	_____	_____
TOTAL COMMITED EXPENDITURES	_____	_____
5. SOMEWHAT DISCRETIONARY:		
Food, Groceries, Etc.	_____	_____
Clothing and Cleaning	_____	_____
Transportation	_____	_____
Medical/Dental Expenses	_____	_____
Housing Supplies/Maintenance	_____	_____

Life Insurance   _____   _____
Current School Expense   _____   _____
Asset Replacement   _____   _____
Other Expenses   _____   _____

TOTAL SOMEWHAT
DISCRECTIONARY   _____   _____

6. VERY DISCRETIONARY:

Vacations, Travel, etc.   _____   _____
Recreational/Entertainment   _____   _____
Contributions, Gifts   _____   _____
Household Furnishings   _____   _____
Education Fund   _____   _____

TOTAL VERY
DISCRETIONARY   _____   _____

TOTAL EXPENSES   _____   _____

Available for Savings/
Investment (Total income
 Less Total Expenses)   _____   _____

Budget Projections
Sample

	Growth Rate	Growth Amount	Current	200X	200X	200X	200X
Employment Income							
Salary-Primary	5.00%	$0	$32,000	$33,600	$35,280	$37,044	$38,896
Salary-Secondary	3.00%	$0	$24,000	$24,72	$25,462	$10,000	$10,300
Total Emploment Income			$56,000	$58,320	$60,742	$47,044	$49,196
Total Other Income			$0	$0	$0	$0	$0
Total Income			$56,000	$58,320	$60,742	$47,044	$49,196
Income Taxes							
Income Taxes	0.00%	$0	$5,300	$5,800	$6,300	$4,300	$4,500
Social Security	0.00%	$0	$4,400	$4,700	$5,000	$3,800	$4,000
Total Income Taxes			$9,700	$10,500	$11,300	$8,100	$8,500
Committed Expenditures							
Housing (Morgage/Rent)	0.00%	$0	$3,600	$3,600	$3,600	$3,600	$3,600
Condo Fee	0.00%	$0	$960	$960	$960	$960	$960
Utilities & Phone	3.00%	$0	$2,400	$2,472	$2,546	$2,623	$2,701
Real Estate Taxes	0.00%	$0	$1,200	$1,200	$1,200	$1,200	$1,200
School Loan	0.00%	$0	$1,200	$1,200	$1,200	$1,200	$1,200
Property & Liability Insurance	3.00%	$0	$2,400	$2,472	$2,546	$2,623	$2,701
Car Loan	0.00%	$0	$3,600	$3,600	$3,600	$3,600	$3,600
Total Committed Expenditures			$15,360	$15,504	$15,652	$12,206	$12,362
Somewhat Discretionary							
Food, Groceries,	3.00%	$0	$5,196	$5,352	$5,512	$5,678	$5,848
Clothing / Cleaning	3.00%	$0	$1,000	$1,030	$1,061	$1,093	$1,126
Transportation	3.00%	$0	$1,800	$1,854	$1,910	$1,967	$2.026
Medical / Dental	3.00%	$0	$1,200	$1,236	$1,273	$3,000	$3,090
Housing Supplies/ Maintenance	3.00%	$0	$300	$309	$318	$328	$338
Life Insurance	0.00%	$0	$480	$480	$480	$480	$480
Asset Replacement	0.00%	$0	$2,400	$2,400	$2,400	$2,400	$2,400
Other Expenses	0.00%	$0	$2,400	$2,400	$2,400	$2,400	$2,400
Total Somewhat Discretionary			$14,776	$15,061	$15,354	$17,346	$17,708

	Growth Rate	Growth Amount	Current	200X	200X	200X	200X
Very Discretionary							
Vacations, Travel, etc.	3.00%	$0	$2,400	$2,472	2,546	$2,623	$2,701
Recreation/ Entertainment	3.00%	$0	$1,800	$1,854	$1,910	$1,967	$2,026
Charitable Contributions	0.00%	$0	$5,600	$5,600	$5,600	$4,700	$4,900
Household Furnishings	0.00%	$0	$1,200	$1,200	$1,200	$1,200	$1,200
Total Very Discretionary			$11,000	$11,126	$11,256	$11,490	$10,827
Total Expenses			$50,836	$52,191	$53,562	$48,142	$49,397
Available for Savings/ Investment			$5,164	$6,129	$7,180	$-1,098	$-201

Goals and Objectives

Few people think of writing down their goals and objectives. Yet goals are one of the most powerful motivating forces known to man. In his book *A Strategy for Daily Living* (New York: Free Press, 1973), Dr. Ari Kiev of Cornell Medical Center states, "With goals people can overcome confusion and conflict over incompatible values, contradictory desires, and frustrated relationships with friends and relatives, all of which often result from the absence of rational life strategies."

He goes on to say, "Observing the lives of people who have mastered adversity, I have repeatedly noted that they have established goals and, irrespective of obstacles, sought with all of their effort to achieve them. From the moment they fixed an objective in their mind and decided to concentrate all their energies on a specific goal, they begin to surmount the most difficult odds."

The purpose of this worksheet is to assist you in outlining for your life goals. While it concentrates on financial goals, you'll also want to compartmentalize your life and your goals into such topics as business and professional goals, family relationship goals, retirement goals, and spiritual goals.

Where would you like to be in terms of financial security within the next five years?

_____

_____

_____

_____

_____

_____

_____

_____

_____

_____

_____

_____

_____

List your financial obligations, dividing them into the present and the future.

Present	Future
_____	_____
_____	_____
_____	_____
_____	_____
_____	_____
_____	_____

Time Value of Money[*]

Age	Early Saver Investment	Value	Late Starter Investment	Value
35	5,000	5,425	0	0
36	5,000	11,311	0	0
37	5,000	17,698	0	0
38	5,000	24,627	0	0
39	5,000	32,145	0	0
40	5,000	40,302	0	0
41	5,000	49,153	0	0
42	5,000	58,756	0	0
43	5,000	69,175	0	0
44	5,000	80,480	0	0
45	0	87,321	7,500	8,138
46	0	94,744	7,500	16,967
47	0	102,797	7,500	26,546
48	0	111,534	7,500	36,940
49	0	121,015	7,500	48,218
50	0	131,301	7,500	60,454
51	0	142,462	7,500	73,730
52	0	154,571	7,500	88,134
53	0	167,710	7,500	103,763
54	0	181,965	7,500	120,721
55	0	197,432	7,500	139,119
56	0	214,214	7,500	159,082
57	0	232,422	7,500	180,741
58	0	252,178	7,500	204,242
59	0	273,613	7,500	229,740
60	0	296,870	7,500	257,405
61	0	322,104	7,500	287,422
62	0	349,483	7,500	319,991
63	0	379,189	7,500	355,328
64	0	411,420	7,500	393,668
65	0	446,390	7,500	435,267

[*]Assuming 8.5%

The Pros and Cons
of Premarital Agreements

Prenuptial agreements are rarely recommended in first marriages unless considerable wealth is brought into the union by one party, although attorneys routinely recommend such agreements to clients embarking on a second marriage. The premarital agreement is used as a means of protecting the financial welfare of children as well as being a means of addressing financial aspects of a second marriage which may not have been considered by the participants.

Many state laws exist to regulate property ownership. In some states known as community property states, all property is presumed to be owned in common, with exceptions for property which is brought into the marriage. However, all property accumulated during the marriage is generally thought of as owned by each equally. There are also federal laws governing pension plans to be taken into consideration in a second marriage.

Having a marital agreement does not mean the new spouse is left without support. To the contrary, many agreements provide for specific assets to be given to the surviving spouse. Life insurance policies can be taken out for the benefit of the new spouse, and there are other means of support which are limited only by the parties' creativity and assets. For example, some agreements provide for increasing marital bequests for each year the parties are married. It is important to emphasize that formulating a premarital agreement it is not a predictor that the marriage will fail. To the contrary, it can avoid problems that could *cause* the marriage to fail.

One of the most compelling arguments offered by Christians opposed to premarital agreements is that they violate biblical principles. In Genesis we are told God made husband and wife to be one flesh. This is a lifetime union between a man and a woman. Treating the money that comes into the family as "my money" rather than "our money" is inconsistent with the "one flesh" idea.

On the other hand, the Hebrew law of inheritance did not provide for the widow. She was almost always considered a part of the estate itself. Of course, this is not true under the New Covenant. The Bible does command us, though, to take care of our family and relatives. Therefore. when either spouse has children from a prior marriage, the dissolution of the marriage whether—by divorce or death—could destroy the inheritance of those children.

It would then seem that each couple, depending upon their marital and financial circumstances, should openly discuss the pros and cons of having a marital agreement. Unless agreed upon by both, it probably is not a good idea. If one party is insistent, the marriage may already be doomed.

To support the thought that this is actually a form of financial planning for a second marriage, let's look at some issues that could be discussed in such an agreement:

- Who will be responsible for pre-existing debts?
- What are the obligations of support that the new husband has?
- Describe which will be the marital home and who will pay the expenses of the home.
- Will each party be responsible for maintaining the cost of other residences or vacation homes?
- Who will be obligated to pay for medical expenses?
- Who will be the attorney-in-fact for powers of attorney and health care powers of attorney?
- If there is a future divorce, will each party waive alimony and release any property claims upon the other spouse?
- Will each party acknowledge property ownership and make full disclosure of such property?
- Will the parties elect to file joint income tax returns and joint gift tax returns?
- If joint tax returns are filed, will there be a provision for determination of each party's tax liability?

- There may or may not be a provision that either party may make voluntary transfers of property to the other notwithstanding any provision of the agreement.

These are only some of the considerations of having a premarital agreement in the event of a second marriage. If such an agreement is drawn, both parties must make full disclosure of their financial assets as well as be represented by their own individual attorney. Also, be aware that each state has different laws, so you should consult a competent attorney in this matter.

College Savings Plans

1. **Coverdell Education Savings Accounts**—This is a savings plan permitted by the Internal Revenue Code so that $2,000 per year can be put aside for a child's education. It is not deductible for income tax purposes, but the earnings accrue tax-free. It is also permitted to use withdrawals for certain elementary and secondary education expenses. The plan provides great flexibility in that the account owner is allowed to change beneficiaries up until the designated beneficiary attains age thirty at which point any assets left in the account must be distributed. It should also be noted that anyone can contribute to these accounts. For example, grandparents could set up Coverdell accounts for their grandchildren. In many cases, one of the parents is designated as the owner of the account. The only limitation is that only $2,000 per child can be contributed in any calendar year. There are also income limitations of the donor to be observed.

2. **Section 529 Plans**—The name of the plan is taken from the Code Section in the Internal Revenue Code that permits these accounts to be set up. They allow people to contribute toward a child's college education in greater amounts than the Coverdell Education Savings Accounts. Like the Coverdell plan, these are not deductible for income tax purposes, but unlike the Coverdell there are no income limitations. Section 529 plans are offered by every state, usually in two varieties: (1) the Prepaid Tuition Plan, and (2) a College Savings Plan. Under the Prepaid Tuition Plan the person buys units at the current market rate

of tuition which can be used in the future to pay for a student's college tuition. Under the College Savings Plan the contributions are invested (usually in mutual funds) more frequently by the states in prescribed portfolios, depending upon the age of the child.

For the more affluent person, Section 529 Plans offer many advantages. As with Coverdell they can be set up by anyone for the benefit of the child. The contributions are subject to gift tax if they exceed the annual exclusion amount (currently $12,000 per year). However, special provisions exist permitting you to pay ahead up to five years' worth of annual exclusions without having to pay any gift tax on the excess.

It also should be noted that parents, grandparents, or whoever can invest in any state plan. It does not have to be the student's state of residence. This gives you the ability to shop for the best performing plan, particularly if you are using the savings account approach. There are, of course, many details with respect to these plans, and you should consult with an expert in the field and/or get the specific information from the state involved.

Appendix 2

Sample Letter for Officiating Minister

Dear_____,

I thank you for asking me to participate in your marriage as the officiating minister. This is a time of wonderful blessing for you and your family, and I appreciate the privilege to participate with you.

In response to your questions regarding my participation in the ceremony, a few guidelines have to be set out as to requirements for you, the engaged couple.

I am writing you this letter because in the past I have performed weddings and lost a good deal of money in the process. I do not have the financial resources to travel and provide room and board while away from home without reimbursement, as this would be harmful to my family.

In light of this, I am asking that you assume the following responsibilities:

1. To pay an honorarium for the performing of the ceremony in the amount of
   $_____.

2. If the ceremony is away from my home base, provide a place for me, and if my family is invited, then for my family and me to stay. I would prefer a hotel or motel for privacy.

3. To pay for transportation costs, either mileage if I travel by car, or the price of a ticket on a common conveyance.

4. A provision for meals while I am away from home.

5. To pay for other expenses that may be incurred by me such as car rental, babysitting fees, etc.

I hope that you will understand reasonableness of these requests. Past problems in this area have caused me to write a letter such as this. I will understand if you cannot afford the financial arrangements. If that is the case, I cannot participate in your wedding.

Thank you for honoring me by asking me to perform your marriage.

Sincerely,

Rev. John Smith

Glossary

amortize. Payments made over a period of time to diminish debt. Amortization refers to payments made against the principal. In a large long-term mortgage very little of the actual debt is amortized in the early years since most of the payment goes toward interest. As the principal diminishes, then more and more of the payment becomes principal and the interest begins to lessen.

asset. An asset is anything that you own whether it is tangible or intangible. For the purposes of financial planning, assets should always be listed at their fair market value.

budget. A budget is an attempt to match income with expenses. Obviously, it is better if the income exceeds the expense, or if the reverse is true, then some trimming must be done. A prolonged state of expenses exceeding income can result in unfortunate consequences.

consolidating debt. It is possible to consolidate school loans through the means of a lender who will pay off the individual loans and in its place leave you with one liability.

dependent. This is anyone who looks to you for financial support.

liabilities. Liabilities refer to financial obligations that you owe to other people. They can be divided into two major categories—short term obligations, which are due within one year, and long-term obligations, which will extend for more than one year.

life insurance. Life insurance is simply insurance on the life of an individual. The amount of life insurance is determined by the loss that would be created in earnings through the death of that individual. Life insurance comes in essentially two forms.

level premium term, which is preferred by many financial planners. This is term policy for a period of years such as 10, 15 or 20. The premiums are added together and then averaged out over the life of the policy. Therefore, instead of having a constantly increasing premium as you do with term insurance, level premium term stays the same during the life of the policy.

market value. The price that a willing buyer would pay to a willing seller.

net worth. Net worth is essentially an accounting equation: Assets − Liabilities = Net Worth. Obviously, assets should exceed liabilities to leave you with a positive net worth. However, in some instances—for example, couples starting in marriage at an early age with heavy school debt—could find themselves in a position of having a negative net worth. Such a condition should get your attention and result in a plan to turn the corner and have assets which exceed your liabilities. This can be accomplished through good budgeting and hard work.

permanent insurance and results in a premium being arrived at by the insurance company based upon actuarial computations. In this form of insurance, the policy owner pays a premium which consists of mortality expenses, administrative expenses, and a plus amount added which will be invested by the insurance company and result in cash value for you at some appropriate time. This is a very expensive type of insurance and in most cases is not the most desirable, particularly for younger couples starting out.

term life is insurance provided on the life of an individual, with the premium determined by the mortality expense of the company and its administrative expenses. This the cheapest form of life insurance.

umbrella policy. This is an excess liability insurance policy usually sold by the same company that insures your house and automobile. It is sold in increments of one million dollars of coverage. Recommended amounts of insurance begin at the minimum of $1 million and can rise to $2 or $3 million depending on the circumstances of each individual. In view of our litigious society, it essential that everyone carry an umbrella policy.